I0158712

Alone

A Musical Dramedy

Book and Lyrics

By Mike Daniel

Music by Leinad Ekim
and Mike Daniel

Absidy Publishing Company ™
Anaheim, CA

Musical Numbers
Act I
I Need a Trash Can..............Reppar, Ekatsim, ENSEMBLE
Sid Lexic, You're So Great.........…..……….ENSEMBLE
Alone..…...Sid
Critical Critique A...…...Quartet
Something New...…...Sid
British Desserts...…............Rona
Rehearsal A.....................…...………..Rona, ENSEMBLE
The Tyrant of Broadway...........………......…...ENSEMBLE
Critical Critique B..…...Quartet
I've Got It All Planned Out........................…...………...Sid
Connection..…....Sid, Rona
Goggily Gossip.....................…..…………Sophie, Terence
Rehearsal B...................……………….………Ensemble
Poor Sid..…...Rona
I Would Rather Be Alone....................................………Sid
Act I Finale...…...COMPANY

Act II
Rehearsal C...………ENSEMBLE
What Was She Thinking?...........................ENSEMBLE
Have I Had It All Wrong?....................................………Rona
Maybe This One Will Be Good...........................Quartet
Mr. E.A. Poe..........................Rona, Rob, ENSEMBLE
Critical Critique C.......................................…....Quartet
I Hate This Song.......................................……Young Sid
Breakdown...........................…..……………ENSEMBLE

Alone was first performed on Thursday, August 21st by the Aloha Performing Arts Company at the Hualalai Academy Bridge Room in Kailua-Kona, Hawaii. The production was directed by Josh Hupp. Musical direction was by Mike Daniel and vocal direction was by Malia Lugo. Lighting/tech was by Marvin Keith. The cast was as follows:

Sid Lexic..Josh Hupp
Rona Exic................................Shanna Westreich
Mosni Niac..................................Sasha Freivalds
Sophie...Rise Lugo
Allison......................................Christi Halvorsen
Terrence.......................................Roxanne Fox
Barry.......................................Gunnar Freivalds
Rob Ing...Arlene Araki
Sab Tard...Tom Daniel
Reppar...Roxanne Fox
Ekatsim....................................Chelsea Cundiff
Tuls...Geppina Scrigna
Sarrah Sment...........................Christi Halvorsen
Deen Sex.............................Mortimer Duckman
Ton Alent.................................Gunnar Freivalds
Pianist................................Bernaldo Evangelista
Maid..Jennifer York
Piano Teacher.......................Bernaldo Evangelista
Young Sid.....................................Roxanne Fox
Sid's Mother................................Robin Hurlbut
Godi Ess......................................Chelsea Cundiff
Chorus........................Karli Lawson, Jim Bristow,
Roseanne Bristow

Cast of Characters

Number Ones:

Sid Lexic: An eccentric musical theater composer always looking for new, innovative theatrical concepts. For reasons unknown until the second act, Sid is unable to move the fingers in his right hand.

Mosni Niac: The only reporter that Sid trusts enough to interview him.

Rona Exic: The female lead of "Poe: The Musical" and Sid's lover.

Number Twos:

The Quartet (Sophie, Allison, Terrence, Barry): A group of people on the street who read the various articles about Sid's shows and life, providing musical interludes for some scene changes.

Rob Ing: A Chinese man cast as Edgar Allen Poe in "Poe: The Musical."

Sab Tard: A backer for "Poe: The Musical."

Number Threes:

Reppar: The star of Sid's musical, "I Need a Trash Can"

Ekatsim: The female lead of "I Need a Trash Can"

Tuls: One of Sid's many short-lasting flings

Lounge Pianist: The pianist at the bar where Sid and Mosni meet

Sarrah Sment, Deen Sex, Ton Alent: Auditioners for "Poe: The Musical"

Pianist, Maid: A pair of Irish hunchbacks. The pianist plays for Sid's auditions and rehearsals, the Maid cleans his house, against his wishes.

Characters of Sid's Past: Sid's piano teacher, Young Sid, Sid's mother, Teenage Sid, Godi Ess

The Voice of Odep Philé

Settings
The Stage: Sid's shows are performed with little or no scenery.

Sid's Appartment: A sofa, a bed, TV. Nothing complex.

The Lounge: Two sofas, a coffee table.

A stand-up piano is blocked at stage right in all scenes. The stage piano parts can be played by the piano player in the pit band with the actors miming playing the piano. On the stage, it's used as an audition/rehearsal piano. In Sid's apartment, it is Sid's personal piano. In the lounge, a piano-bar player plays background music under the scenes. It is also the piano used in Sid's flashback scenes.

A Note on Staging
There are several ways that *Alone* could be staged. It could be done as a huge, full production musical, or it could be done with little or no sets at all. A bare-stage production would lend an interesting layer to a production as another level of commentary on the bleakness of Sid and Rona's lifestyles. While a full-blown production could also be lots of fun! It is entirely up to your artistic taste and/or budget.

To Natalie, Nani, Roxy and the rest of my first fan club.

Act I

(We open on an early morning street scene; music under. A BUM [Played by REPPAR] who is sitting on the ground pulls out a stick of gum, unwraps it, and puts it in his mouth. Looking for a place to deposit the wrapper he asks a few passersby—who ignore him—if they have a trash can.)

Reppar: *(fed up with being ignored, jumps up and sings)*

> Yo, mo' fu's, the word on the street is
> I need a trash can and I gotta take a wiz.
> So listen up coz, I'm in a real bind,
> My bladder's burstin', and a can I gotta find.
> That's right!

I need a trash can!	Vagrants: *(sing)*
	Trash, trash, trash can!
I need a trash can!	Trash, trash, trash can!
I need a trash can!	Trash, trash, trash can!
I need a trash can!	Trash, trash, trash can!

Passer-by Woman [Ekatsim]: *(ad-libbing vocally, sings)*

> Will someone please help this poor man out?
> Can't you see he's a desperate li'l scout?
> The man needs a can, so give the can a man—
> I mean—
> He's starting to wheeze, and it makes me wanna
>   shout

He needs a trash can!	Women: *(sing, operatic)*
	He needs a trash can!

1

Reppar: Sing it girl!
He needs a trash can! Women:
He needs a trash can!
Reppar: That's right!
Reppar and Women:
I/he need(s) a trash can!
Ekatsim:
So give the man a
can!

A Passer-by Man: *(pointing to a nearby trash can)* Hey, dumb-ass, there's a can right over there.

(Awkward pause as REPPAR throws away his trash.)

Reppar: *(spoken)* Yo, everybody! Never mind!
(sings)
That's right!
I don't need a trash can!
Ekatsim: *(sings)*

He doesn't need a can!
Don't need a trash can!

Listen to the man,
Don't need a trash can!
He don't need a trash can!
'Cause who needs a can?

(Repeat above until SID cuts them off.)

Sid: *(storming on stage from the house)* No, no, no, no, no! Reppar, I need to *feel* your motivation here! Come

on, work with me! Work with me! Help me help me.[*]
Okay, okay, okay. Picture this scene with me, okay?
(music under) It's early morning. You've just woken up
and you're chewing on a piece of gum. But, you don't
have a place to throw the wrapper. Okay, you with me
so far?

Reppar: Ye—

Sid: *(continuing)* Then, you *find* a trash can! The very
trash can you've spent the last five minutes looking for!
It's a miracle! A sign from God! Your trash can has
been found! You have a place to put your trash! *(to the
PIT ORCHESTRA)* Knock it off, we're trying to work
up here!

Members of the Orchestra: Sorry, Sid.

Sid: *(continuing, no music)* Where was I? Okay, you
have a place to put your trash! This is what you have
wanted since you woke up five minutes ago! How do
you feel?

Reppar: Well, I really don't see what the big deal is. It's
just a trash—

Sid: *(interrupting)* No! It's not just a trash can! It's *the*
trash can! *(giving up in frustration)* Actors! *(to
EKATSIM, falsely friendly)* Ekatsim! Beautiful darling!
Splendidly splentacular! Really darling, a marvelous
performance. I honestly was touched. You touched me
so much, I think I'm going to go out and have a lobot-
omy. But I have just one, teensy, weensy, tiny, winey

---

[*] A play on the phrase "Help me help you."

3

little comment. *(suddenly yelling in her ear) GIVE THE CAN A MAN?* What the Hell is that supposed to mean? How can you possibly—in this dimension, mind you—give a man to a can? What would a can want with a man? Is it going to take him out to dinner and buy him flowers? *(throwing up his arms in frustration)* Come on people, work with me here! We open in one week and one of my stars still doesn't understand the great moral significance of having found a trash can while my other star has some strange delusions about the feelings that trash cans have for humans!

(TULS, SID'S current fling, walks up on stage from the house. Like most of his flings, TULS is a skimpy little thing with more on her chest than in her head.)

Tuls: Oh Siddy honey, if we don't go soon we're going to miss the movie, and then we'd just have to go straight home and do whatever.

Sid: *(after a beat)* Right, dear. *(to CAST)* Well, we obviously aren't going to make any more ground with you people tonight, so get on home and at least pretend to work on your parts. *(to TULS as he runs off U.L.)* Wait right here, Becky, I just have to grab some things from the wings.

Tuls: *(correcting)* It's Tuls.

Sid: *(confused)* What?

Tuls: My name is Tuls.

Sid: Oh yeah, right. Becky was last week. Sorry 'bout that honey, I'll be right down.

4

(SID exits U.L. As TULS waits D.L., checking her make-up, the CAST gathers D.R. gossiping. Music under.)

Woman 1: You see that tramp Sid picked up this week?

Man 1: Every week it's another girl with him.

Woman 2: You know, that boy has got to settle down at some point. It's not healthy for a man to stay a bachelor all his life.

Ensemble: *(sings)*
     In all the land of Broadway,
     There's one director who
         stands out among the rest.
     Although we wouldn't go as far
         as to say he's the best.
     All his shows seem to say,
     "Hey, look at me!
     I'm the strangest writer on Broadway today!"

     He's not the king of Broadway,
     But as far as writer/director's go,
         we think that he'll do.
     Who cares if critics write reviews
         that say "Poo"?
     He makes all the broads say,

Tuls: *(from D.L., sings)*
     "Ooh, look at him!
     Wouldn't mind to take him
         to my personal gym!"

Ensemble:
>   Hey, Sid Lexic, you're so great!

Tuls: Your shows make ev'ry muscle
>   in my body girate!

Ensemble & Tuls:
>   But God, you can be a pain in the butt.

Ensemble:
>   If you're looking for a thick plot,
>   You really oughta go and see a Sondheim show.

A Man:
>   I hear that they've revived "Into the Woods."

Ensemble:
>   His shows may not all flow
>   Like liquid foods.

Another Man:
>   But at least he doesn't have
>   chandeliers and helicopters.

Ensemble:
>   His plots may not have a point

Tuls: But with that pointer of his,
>   who needs a plot point?

Another Man:
>   His shows actually make some
>   sense when you're high on a joint...

Ensemble:
>   We here up on the stage
>   Just want to say
>   Hey, Sid Lexic, you're our guy!

Tuls: Your shows make me feel so high!

Ensemble and Tuls:
>But, Sid Lexic,
>Yes, Sid Lexic,
>Hey, Sid Lexic—

(SID enters from U.L. and crosses to TULS.)

Sid: Ready, babe?

Tuls: You betcha, Sid!

Ensemble: *(as SID and TULS exit)*
>God, you can be a pain in the butt!

(Blackout.)

Music Under Scene Change.

At Rise: *(A hotel lounge or bar. A PIANIST sits at the D.R. piano playing "Moonlight Sonata." SID is having an interview with MOSNI NIAC, the only reporter he trusts to interview him. The interview has just started and they're having a laugh over something previously said.)*

Mosni: *(getting down to business, turning on her tape recorder)* Well Sid, if it's all right with you, I'd like to get on with the interview.

Sid: Certainly, Mosni. It's always been a pleasure to be featured in *Mosni Niac Talks Broadway.*

Mosni: Well, thank you Sid. And it's always been an honor to be the only reporter in New York that you'll talk to. Now, tell me about your new rap-opera, *I Need a Trash Can.*

Sid: Well, Mosni, I prefer to call it a Rapera.

Mosni: Ooh, that's catchy.

Sid: Well, thank you. The idea just came to me one night as I was falling asleep. I was trying to think of a new musical form to create and I realized that no one has ever written a rap musical before. And the rest—pardon the cliché—is history.

Mosni: That's just fascinating. Now, you're cast is pretty exceptional as I understand. Your main star is Reppar, who is a *very* big name in the rapping industry.

Sid: Oh yes, I'm working with an exceptional cast. Reppar has all of his lines down perfectly and his supporting actress, Ekatsim, knows her character better than I know myself.

Mosni: That's wonderful to hear. So you're looking forward to opening night next week?

Sid: Oh, I have a very good feeling about this show. As you know, many of my shows—with the exception of *Someone Stole the Beans*—haven't gone over too well with critics. But I'm certain that I *Needs a Trashcan* will be a hit.

Mosni: Well, I certainly wish the best for you. Now, on a more personal note, women all over New York want to know when Sid Lexic will settle down and get into a serious relationship. You are, after all, one of the most eligible bachelor's in the city.

Sid: Well, Mosni, I'm a man who is married to his music and there just isn't room in my life for that kind of relationship.

Mosni: Well, that's too bad. The women of New York will be very sad to hear that.

(SID snaps his fingers and the scene freezes. He steps out of the interview and confronts the audience.)

Sid: Everyone is always on my case about this. No one understands that I actually enjoy being alone. If you ask me, a man's best company is himself. We chose the song we wish to sing, and that's the song we sing. Some people just work better when they're alone.
>
> *(sings)*
> When you're alone
> You're the king of the crowd,
> No ifs ands or buts allowed.
>
> When you're alone
> It's all right if you shout
> And no one cares if you pout.
>
> Take it from me, love's not that grand.
> You'd be better off free!
> Take your own hand, live life alone.
> Then you'll see what is grand.
>
> When you're alone
> You're the head of the pack
> With no one to answer back.

When you're alone
You just answer to you
And not some domineering broad.

When you're alone, you've got it made
No more groans and moans.
You've got the spade when you're alone.
You defend your own barricade!

When you're alone
You've got no commitments
And you can keep your two cents

When you're alone
You at last realize
What's written up there in the skies
(Stepping back into the interview.)
It's better to be alone.

(SID snaps his fingers, unfreezing the scene.)

Sid: *(to MOSNI)* Well, what can I say? I'm just a born bachelor.

(Blackout.)

During Scene Change:
(The QUARTET steps forward into a spotlight, each reading their own newspaper during the scene change. SOPHIE, a ditsy teeny-bopper, reads from Broadway for Teens Magazine; *ALISON, a sophisticated feminist, reads from* The New York Times; *TERENCE, a flamboyant actor, from* Drama Queen Magazine; *and BARRY, a snob, from* The New York Gazette.)

Sophie: *(sings)*
>Sid Lexic's new "Rapera"—

Alison: *(sings)*
>*—I Need a Trash Can—*

Barry: *(sings)*
>—stinks.

Terence: *(sings)*
>—made Lloyd Webber cringe.

Alison:
>—could use some work.

Sophie:
>—is super!!!

Alison:
>It makes me wonder what
>>Broadway is coming to.

Barry: What's next, a Punk Opera?

Terence:
>I think Lexic should really tone it back.

Sophie:
>Eminem says it's the best—and only—
>>musical he's ever seen!!!

Barry: Or maybe *Bin Laden: The Musical*?

Alison:
>Sid should have stuck with
>>his minimalism phase.

Terence:
>It's just not something that
>>Sondheim would write.

Barry: At least his minimalist musicals had points—

Sophie:
>Mister Em says that he's started writing
>>his own rapera, *Bitch, Get My Beer*!!!

Barry: —in the music at least.

Alison:
>It was a rather unpleasant evening.

Terence:
>Completely miserable.

Barry: Unbearable.

All Four:
>I've never seen anything so…
>>I've never seen anything so…

Alison, Terrence, Barry:	Sophie:
…terrible.	…super!!!

At Rise: *(The QUARTET exits as the lights come up on SID'S apartment. Posters of his many flop musicals adorn the walls; e.g.:* Someone Stole the Beans, Smelly Socks, Clinton: The Musical *[or* Elian Gonzales: The Musical]*, The Can of Rotten Tuna at the End of the

Road to Tomorrow, *etc. SID enters carrying a copy of the* New York Times' *review of* I Need a Trash Can. *Crushed, he collapses onto the couch.)*

Sid: *(sings)*
> Look at these reviews.
> Look at these reviews.
> They all think I'm a snooze.
> When will they see
> What I want them to see?
> When can I be
> The writer I want to be.

(He turns on the music box next to the couch and it begins playing Fur Elise. *As it plays, he checks his answering machine.)*

Message #1: Hey Sid, it's Barry. Just read the review in the *Times,* just wanted to call and say I told you so. Later.

Message #2 (Tuls): Hi honey! Did opening night go well? Sorry I couldn't be there, but you know how my boss at the strip club can be. Anyway, call me if you want me to come over later and we can do whatever. Love you!

Message #3 (Mosni): Hey Sid, it's Mosni. Thought you might want someone to talk to—off the record of course—about tonight. Don't let those jackasses ruin your vision. Just keep doing what you know you want to do. Call me.

(The music box stops playing. SID looks at it sadly for a few moments.)

Sid: *(sings)*
> I just want to write something new,
> That will sell lots of tickets.
> That won't make critics yell out "Boo!"
> That won't fill the theater with
> > sounds of crickets.

> People will come from miles to see
> A new show that's written and directed by me.
> My songs will be sung on the radio
> And I will write my autobio.

> But the critics are always there
> Watching every move you make.
> How they make my stomach ache,
> Why, they even criticized my hair!

> I need something new,
> That no one's done before!
> Must be something I can do
> To make the audiences roar.

(Suddenly, as he gets an idea, he jumps up and begins pacing.)
> Of course, I've got it!
> I've really got it!
> My new show!

(spoken, music under)

When in doubt, modernize a Shakespeare tragedy! After all, nothing's more uplifting than a show where everyone dies. But what Shakespeare show is timeless enough to be originally modernized for the first time? Of course! *Romeo and Juliet*! *("America" from* West Side Story *plays softly in the background.)* All right, forget Roy and Julie. Who needs Shakespeare anyway? He's either too depressing or too controversial. Besides, there's other classics out there. What I need is a classic tale about the battle between Good and Evil. Of course! *Jekyll and Hyde! ("This is the Moment" from* Jekyll and Hyde *plays softly in the background.)*

> *(sings)*
> I need something new!
> That no one's done before.
> Must be something I can do
> To make the audiences roar!

(spoken, music under)
I'm on the right track, though. What I need is a thriller, something to shock my audiences into coming again and again! Of course! I'll write a show about a serial killer! *That* hasn't been done before! *("Johanna" from* Sweeney Todd *plays softly in the background.)* Ah, forget it.

> *(sings)*
> Something new!
> I'm on the verge of something new,
> I can feel it!

(spoken)
Perhaps instead of a common killer, I should focus on the story of a famous dictator…of course! *Lenin: The Musical*!

> *(sings)*
> No wait, it sounds too much like
> "Springtime for Hitler and Germany."
> Or, how about
> *Autumn for Bin Laden and Afghanistan?...*

(spoken)
But I'm on the right track, it's clear that I'm looking for a suspense.

(sings)
Of course, I've got it!
I've really got it!
My new show!

Of course, at last, I finally see
(pulling a book off of his bookshelf)
The answer's right in front of me!
I'll write a brand new thrilling show
In honor of the master of suspense:
(holding up the book, a collection of poems by Edgar Allan Poe)
Mister Edgar Allan Poe!

It really makes perfect sense,
Poe will be my masterpiece!
I feel a boost in confidence!
I'll write music to his poems
My songs will be shiny and blue,
Why, some may become anthems!

At last I've found something new!
Something that's never been done!
At last the horizon is blue
And the race will be won!

I'm going to write something new!
My own *I Dreamed a Dream*!
It won't make critics yell out "Boo!"
It will make my fans scream!
I'm going to write something new!
(Blackout.)
Music Under Scene Change

At Rise: *(Auditions for* Poe: The Musical. *A desk is set up D.L. at which SID and a few members of his production team sit. A hunch-backed Irish PIANIST sits at the D.R. piano.)*

Sid: Next!

(SARRAH SMENT steps up on stage.)

Sid: Name and title of what you're performing.

Sarrah: My name is Sarrah[*] Sment and I will be performing "Who Stole My Socks?" from the musical *Smelly Socks*. *(to accompanist)* Key of G, please.

Pianist: Oh, sure missy. I'll just play in whatever key you want. You sure you don't want it in C-flat minor?

Sid: Uh, don't mind him, he's just a little grumpy after having played all day.

Pianist: Well just announce to the world that I'm an alcoholic, why don't you?

Sid: *(ignoring him)* Please continue.

Sarrah: *(sings)*
        Have you seen my socks?
        Someone stole my socks!
        I filled them up with rocks,
        To make them hard to steal,
        But now my socks are gone—

---

[*] Actress should roll the R's in her name as ridiculously long as possible.

17

Sid: *(interrupting)* Uh, Sarah—

Sarrah: *(correcting him)* It's Sarrah.

Sid: Sorry, Sarrah. Um, that song's not from *Smelly Socks,* is it?

Sarrah: Um, no. It's actually a song I wrote.

Sid: I see. Why would you come here and pose it as someone else's?

Sarrah: Well, you see, I was hoping that after I got into the theater community that I could get my work known. I chose *Smelly Socks* because it's a musical that no one knows the music to.

Sid: I see. You wouldn't, by any chance, know who wrote the music for *Smelly Socks*, would you?

Sarrah: Um, some guy named Sid Lexic, I think.

Sid: I see…next!

(Confused, SARRAH walks off stage. DEEN SEX steps up.)

Sid: Name and what song your doing.

Deen: My name is Deen, D-E-E-N, Sex, S-E-X.

Sid: You poor thing.

Deen: I will be performing the song "2002 Catholic Priests."

Pianist: Oh, and I suppose that's a crack against me religion, ain't it?

Deen: *(clearing his throat, sings)*
It's a shitty time to be Catholic
For everywhere you look
You find another nook
Where a priest has put his—

Sid: *(interrupting)* That's a terrible song. Next!

Deen: Hey, you know, I don't have to take this, you know? I was in *Cats* for five years.

Sid: Really? Well, now that just changes everything. *Security!*

(A SECURITY GUARD walks on stage and drags DEEN off kicking and screaming. TON ALENT, an extremely well-built man, steps up.)

Ton: My name is Ton—that's *Ton*, not *Tom*—

Sid: *(aside)* Where do we find these people?

Ton: —and I will be performing "Tomorrow" from *Annie*.

Sid: Next!

(Crushed, TON exits. RONA EXIC steps up, dressed rather revealingly.)

Sid: Well, hello there. What's your name and phone nu—I mean what's your name and the title of the song you'll be performing today?

Rona: My name is Rona Exic, that's *Exic* without an "L."

Sid: That's interesting. I've never met someone with a name so similar to mine.

Rona: Yeah, I get that a lot.

Sid: Well, what will you be performing for us today?

Rona: I'll be singing the title song from your musical *British Desserts. (to PIANIST)* Key of E-flat, please.

Pianist: *(almost drooling)* Would you like that in C-sharp major, instead, lass?

Rona: No, E-flat will be fine, thank you.

Pianist: As you wish, lassy. Anything for a charmin' young woman such as yourself.

Rona: *(sings)*
> I've had lots of men
> And I've begun to see
> That once a man has been with me
> He comes again…and again.
>
> Some wrote me poetry
> To get into my head.
> Other bought me jewelry

To get into my bed.

After all these men,
The break-ups…stop to hurt.
But again, and again…and again,
Through the men who taught me
And the men who thought me
A flirt,
The men I remem-
-ber are the ones who bought me…
Dessert.

*(Fantasy takes over from reality as three CHORUS
GIRLS enter and sing back-up.)*

Rona: Chorus Girls:
   Presents are fine,   Fine,
   Most of the time,   Time,
   Just not in excess.   Just not in excess!
   Now don't get me wrong,   Wrong,
   I do like gifts,   Like gifts,
   But I have to confess   Have to confess!

   When in the presence of too many presents
   A girl can get lost in all of the nonsense!

   Diamonds are nice,   Diamonds are nice!
   To an extent,
   Can't refuse
   a guy who has spent.   A guy who is spent!
   But when he
   buys you mice,   Buys you mice,
   You really must see   You really must see!

   When a lover buys you a mouse for a pet

You suddenly have two rodents
        that need to be fed.

To summarize,
Presents are nice   Presents are nice
Once in a while,   Once in a while.
But if you wanna
Make me smile,   Make her smile,
You'd better buy
Me dessert!   Buy her dessert!

Sundays are fine,
And choc'late's divine.
But if I had to wish for my favorite dish,
I'd say I'd have to pick the Brittish's spotted
        dick!

All Four:
        Oh yeah, we love a good spotted dick
Rona: Chorus Girls:
        With its creamy filling!   Creamy filling!
        I could never get sick
        Of that scrumptious titillating feeling
        In my mouth!

(RONA belly dances in front of the audition desk as the CHORUS GIRLS take over.)

Chorus Girls:
        We just need our
        Spotted dick!

        Once you've had your
        First spotted dick,
        You can never go back!

Four or five or six times a week
Rona:
I get a craving for that spotted dick attack!

Chorus Girls:
God, we love our
Spotted dick!
Rona: I'll have one again…and again!

*(Reality takes over fantasy as RONA reaches her climax
and the CHORUS GIRLS begin to fade out of the
picture.)*

Rona:
Can't get enough of that stuff!
All I want is more and more!
I may be a social bore,
But I don't care as long as you—quick,
Give me a taste of your spotted dick!
Oh, yesss!!!!

Sid: When can you start rehearsals?

(Blackout.)

Music Under Scene Change.

At Rise: *(First rehearsal for* Poe. *The title role is
performed by ROB ING, a Chinese man. RONA is cast
as POE'S wife, LENORE. ROB is sitting at a writing
desk scribbling away at paper as the CHORUS sings
behind him, drifting in and out of shadows in abstract
choreography. The piano is set up D.R. and our friend,
the hunch-backed Irish PIANIST sits at it.)*

23

Chorus: *(sings)*
>Hear the sledges with the bells—
>>Silver bells!
>What a world of merriment their melody
>>foretells!
>How they tinkle, tinkle, tinkle,
>>In the icy air of night!
>While the stars that oversprinkle
>All the heavens seem to twinkle
>>With a crystalline delight;
>Keeping time, time, time,
>In a sort of Runic rhyme,
>To the tintinnabulation that so musically wells
>From the bells, bells, bells, bells,
>>Bells, bells, bells—
>From the jingling and the tinkling of the—

Rona (As LENORE): *(interrupting his writing)* Edgar, dear, why don't you come to bed?

Rob (As POE): *(annoyed)* Not now, Lenore, I'm working!

Rona: *(pouting seductively)* But you're always working, Eddy. Why don't you come to bed and I'll jingle and tinkle your bells for you…

Rob: Lenore, not now.

Rona: Nevermore for Lenore?
>*(frustrated, sings)*
>The ring is on my hand,
>>And the wreath is on my brow;
>Satins and jewels grand
>Are all at my command

And I am happy now.

And my lord he loves me well;
                    But when first he breathed his vow
I felt my bosom swell—
For the words rang as a knell,
And the voice seemed *his* who fell
In the battle down the dell,
                    And who is happy—

Rob: *(interrupting, out of character, to SID who is in the house)* Excuse me, Sid, but I have just one suggestion regarding script.

(The CAST all holds there breath and watches SID warily as he walks up on stage and crosses to ROB.)

Sid: And what might that be, Rob?

Rob: *(gulping nervously)* Well, just that Poe never married a woman named Lenore. He married his cousin, Virginia Clemm who, I might add, was fourteen years younger than himself.

Pianist: He's right you know. Although I must say that I resent the tone of disapproval regarding incestual pedophilia.

(Awkward silence as the CAST waits for the explosion.)

Sid: That's a very good point, Rob. *(The CAST cast confused glances at each other.)* That is a rather troublesome historic detail. *(getting an idea)* Wait! I've got it! Okay, I think I've got a "what if?" What if Lenore is Poe's *imaginary* mistress? You know, like a delusion or something! Thank you, Rob, for your suggestion. *(ROB nods sheepishly)* You know, you've all done such a wonderful job tonight, why don't you all go home early. *(The CAST looks at him in disbelief.)*

Pianist: *(cautiously)* You're not joking, are you? Are you feeling all right, laddy? Did you knock your head on the door handle a few too many times? I know I've done that my own share of times, yessy.

Sid: No, no. Go on home to your families. I'll make sure that you get paid for the full two-hour rehearsal.

(As the CAST tries to figure out what's going on, SID approaches RONA who is standing D.L., checking her make-up. He nervously tries approaching her several times, but backs off each time.)

Solo 1: *(sings)*
      Something's wrong…

Solo 2: *(sings)*
      Something's not right…

Solo 3: *(sings)*
      This isn't Sid's song…

Solo 4: *(sings)*
      Sid's happy, he's usually snappy…

All Four:
      We should be bubbling with delight.

Ensemble: *(sings)*
      What can make the Tyrant of Broadway

So happy and gay?

Rob: *(speaks)* I thought Sid was straight?

Solo 5: *(sings)*
>Do you think that he's high?…

Solo 6: *(sings)*
>I've never seen Sid on drugs…

Solo 7: *(sings)*
>I might have seen him talking to some thugs…

Solo 5:
>Do you think he's gonna die?

Solos 6&7:
>Who Sid? No…
>Well, maybe so…

Rob: *(speaks)* Hey guys, maybe he's—

Ensemble: *(cutting-off ROB, sings)*
>What can make the Tyrant of Broadway
>Have a good day?

Solo 1:
>Maybe his mom died…

Solo 2:
>I know for *that* bitch he wouldn't have cried…

Solo 6:
>You shouldn't say that about his mother…

Solo 2:

   Sid's mother isn't just another mother…

Solo 3:

   Besides he
   Hates her more than we
   Do.

Rob: *(speaks)* Hey guys, maybe he's—

Ensemble: *(cutting-off ROB again)*
   Now don't get us wrong,
   Sid really is great.
   But for him to celebrate—
   Something doesn't belong.

Rob: Hey, do you think he's in—

Solo 4: *(cutting-off ROB)*
   Maybe he's got the clap—

Solo 5:

   That wouldn't normally
   Make someone hap-
   -py…

Solo 5:

   But Sid, after all, is an odd chap…

Rob: Hey guys, do you think—

Ensemble: *(cutting-off ROB again, sings)*
   You can never tell
   If he's under a spell
   Or just simply dotty.

Rob: *(losing his patience, yells out)* Hey guys!!! *(silence as he has their attention.)* Do you think he's in love?

Ensemble: *(sings)*
> In love? Sid?
> No, not he,
> That couldn't be it.

(At D.L., SID finally summons the courage and approaches RONA. The CAST watches anxiously.)

Sid: *(nervously)* Uh, Rona…

Rona: Yes, Sid?

Sid: Well, I was, uh, wondering if…well if you'd like to join me for dinner tonight?

Rona: Why yes, Sid. I'd be delighted.

Sid: Really? I mean…well, shall we?

(They leave arm in arm as the CAST watches dumb-founded.)

Rob: Told you so.

During Scene Change:
(The QUARTET enters a spotlight as the lights go out and read from their respective newspapers during the scene change.)

Sophie: *(sings)*
>Sid's casting decisions for
>>his new upcoming show—

Barry: *(sings)*
>—*Poe:*—

Terence: *(sings)*
>—*The Musical*—

Alison: *(sings)*
>—could be described as—

Sophie:
>—super!!!

Alison:
>—vastly inadequate.

Terence:
>—queer.

Barry: —pathetic.

Terrence:
>He's cast a Chinese man
>As the famous American poet!

Sophie:
>Rob Ing is, like, *so* cute!!!

Terrence:
>Now, don't get me wrong,
>I'm not trying to get in trouble
>With the Equity Board, here—

Alison:
> And Rona Exic is little more than
> A skimp in tramp's clothing.

Terrence:
> —But give me a break.

Barry: Whatever happened to great shows
> Like *Amadeus*?

Sophie:
> Overall—

Alison:
> —In regards to *Poe: The Musical*—

Terrence:
> —when it comes to town—

Barry: —I would recommend—

Alison:
> —that you spend your evening—

Terrence:
> —watching *Will and Grace.*

Alison:
> —curled up with a good book.

Barry: —watching *Frasier.*

Sophie:
> —talking on the phone!

(spoken, as the others leave, annoyed)
Wait, what was the question?

(The QUARTET exits.)

At Rise: *(Lights Come up on SID'S apartment. Grunting and cursing can be heard off-stage along with the clanging of pots and pans. SID and RONA enter laughing. A hunch-backed Irish MAID runs into the living room from the off-stage kitchen U.R. yelling and cursing at SID.)*

Maid: You! How many times do I tell you? I don't do dishes! Every time I come, the dishes are all over the place!

Sid: *(defending himself as she tries to beat him with a frying pan)* What are you talking about? Who are you? I don't have a maid! Get off me!

Maid: What? You mean you're not Mr. Dunmeier of 150 Massachusetts Avenue Apartment Number 4?

Sid: No, I'm Sid Lexic and we're not even in Massachusetts—this is New York City, you crazy loon.

Maid: Oh, crappy. I done it again, I did. Well beat me over the head with a broken spoon. My apologies, laddy.

Sid: *(as she begins to leave)* Excuse me, your husband isn't, by any chance, a pianist?

Maid: Now how did you know that?

Sid: Oh, just a hunch.

Maid: *(leaving)* What a strange young lad, you are.

Sid: *(embarrassed, apologizing to RONA)* That doesn't normally happen.

Rona: *(trying to stop from grinning)* I should hope not.

Sid: *(indicating the sofa)* Here, have a seat. I'll go get some champagne.

(Sitting on the sofa, RONA notices the piano.)

Rona: That's a lovely piano. Do you play often?

Sid: *(stiffly, while he fixes the drinks)* No, not really. I used to, but lately I've just used it for plunking out the melodies for my music.

(She notices that while SID fixes the drinks, he avoids using his right hand.)

Rona: What's wrong with your hand?

Sid: *(bringing the drinks over on a tray)* What?

Rona: Your hand. You haven't been using your right hand all night. You opened the door for me with your left hand, you wouldn't hold hands with me if I was standing to your right, and you just fixed the drinks without using your right hand.

Sid: *(awkwardly)* Oh, that. Well, I had an accident when I was a child, and I haven't been able to move my

33

fingers since. It's really nothing. I've learned to get along without it.

(Sensing that he doesn't want to talk about it any further, she drops the subject and, taking a sip of wine, notices the music box and turns it on.)

Rona: Mmm, Beethoven. I don't know what it is, but something about his music just speaks to me, you know what I mean?

Sid: I know exactly what you mean. Anyway, continue telling me about…Bob was it?

Rona: Barry. Well there's really not much else to tell. Just like all the men that came after him. With Barry I realized that I could get whatever I wanted from men just by using my body to give them what they wanted. Since him, I've basically just been bouncing from man to man. Once I got what I wanted out of one man, I moved on to the next. I guess I just never found the need for love. What about you? What was your first fling like?

Sid: Goddi? Pretty much the same story. I was at a pretty miserable state when Goddi came into my life. My father had died a few years earlier. My uncle Ben who had…"adopted" me had just died. I was desperate for someone to connect with, and Goddi was the first person to come along. Long story short, she dumped me after a month, broke my heart and convinced me that I was better off taking care of myself.

Rona: What a pair we are, huh? Two completely dysfunctional adults. *(toasting)* To dysfunction.

Sid: *(clinking her glass with his)* To dysfunction.

(RONA leans over to kiss him on the lips. SID snaps his fingers and as the scene freezes, he steps out of the scene to confront the audience.)

Sid: *(sings)*
  What is this?
  What is this about?
  This cannot happen!
  I've got a plan,
  I've got it all planned out!

  I need to create,
  I need to create a great
  New show!
  With the life that I lead,
  There's no room for a mate!
  I go where I need
  To go!

  I made the decision years ago
  To live life all alone.
  There is no other way to go
  When you've got dreams to see grown.

  How can this happen?
  Why is it now?
  Now that my dreams are just within reach?
  I'm not ready for that final vow.
  I've still got dreams to seek!

  I live alone
  Because it's simpler.

A family would mean
Abandoning my dream!
The more mouths to feed,
The harder to satisfy *your* need.

(RONA unfreezes and gently guides him back to the couch.)

Sid: *(gazing into her eyes, sings)*
But when I look into her face,
I feel my convictions start to unlace.
Have I really had it wrong?
Are there really other songs
That I could sing?
I thought I had it all planned out.

(They kiss. Blackout.)

At Rise: *(The next morning. SID wakes with RONA in his arms.)*

Sid: *(watching her sleep, sings)*
I don't want to be alone.
Never again will I say
"Alone is the way for me."
At last, I finally see,
I'm in love.
I was a fool when I said
Love, for me, is dead.
(as RONA wakes)
Please let me into your world.

Connection,
I'm finally connecting
With someone.

It's time I start correcting
My life.

Connection,
I can't believe
I found you.
I'm happier when I'm
Around you.

Rona: *(sings)*
Connection,
I think I'm falling
In love.
I hear my fate calling
To me.

Connection,
These are feelings
I have
Never known.

Sid: Maybe life shouldn't be spent
Alone!

Together:
I can't believe I finally found someone.
For so long I've been on my own.
But now I know I'm not alone.

Sid: Dawn is rising and you're my shining sun!

Together:
Connection,
I can't believe
I found you!

I'm happier when I'm
Around you!

Connection,
I'm finally connecting
With someone!
It's time to start correcting
My life!
Please let me into your world.

(They embrace.)

During Scene Change:
*(As the lights dim out, SOPHIE and TERENCE step
into a spotlight reading out of the tabloids.)*

Sophie: *(sings)*
      Scandal!

Terence: *(sings)*
      Goggily gossip!

Together:
      Sid and "Rona the Moaner"[*]

Sophie:
      How could he leave me like this?

Terence:
      What a scallerous scandal!

Sophie:
      I have his pictures plastered

---

[*] Pronounced with a silent "R"

All over my room!

Terence:
       What rumferdescent rumors!

Sophie:
       I fall asleep every night
       To a tape recording of his voice.

Terence:
       What—*(to SOPHIE, shocked)* What?

Sophie: *(spoken)* Oh, is that too much?

Terence: *(spoken)* That's what we in show biz call an obstinatious obsession, honey.

Sophie: *(embarrassed)* Sorry.

Terence: Don't worry, sister, we all have them at some point. Me, I couldn't keep my mind off of the guy who played Newman on *Seinfeld* when I was your age.

Sophie: *(disgusted)* That's…interesting…

Terence: Come on, let me buy you some cocoa.

Sophie: Thanks.

(They exit together as the lights fade out.)

Music Under Remaining Scene Change.

39

Through Darkness: *(The ticking of a tock can be heard through the darkness.)*

At Rise: *(Lights come up on a rehearsal for* Poe. *A little more than a month has passed and the show is nearing production; a pit orchestra has been added and the cast no longer use their scripts. As before, ROB is sitting at his desk as POE and the CHORUS darts in and out of shadows behind him as they sing what he writes.)*

Chorus: *(sings)*
> Hear the mellow wedding bells,
> > Golden bells!
> What a world of happiness their harmony
> > foretells!
> Through the balmy air of night
> How they ring out their delight!
> From the molten-golden notes,
> > And all in tune,
> What a liquid ditty floats
> To the turtle-dove that listens, while she gloats
> > On the moon!
> Oh, from out the sounding cells
> What a gush of euphony voluminously wells!
> > How it swells!
> > How it dwells!
> On the future! how it tells
> Of the rapture that impels
> To the swinging and the ringing
> Of the bells, bells, bells,
> Of the bells, bells, bells, bells,
> > Bells, bells, bells—
> To the rhyming and the chiming of the bells!

(SID applauding as he walks on stage.)

Sid: Wonderful! Simply wonderful! I'm overcome with joy! Ladies and gentlemen, we have a very special guest watching on today, Mister Sab Tard! Come on, Sab, come on up here! *(SAB walks up on stage from the house.)* Mister Tard is a prospective backer for our show.

Sab: *(politely, but unsuccessfully, hiding his lack of enthusiasm)* Well, thank you, Sid. And I'd like to congratulate you and Rona on the engagement.

Sid and Rona: *(blushing)* Thank you.

Sid: As you know, Mister Tard, we've been in rehearsal for over a month now and—with the proper backing—we should be ready to open within the next month.

Sab: Well, yes. Of course, I'm not sure, as of yet, whether or not I'm going to back your…little performance. Listen, Sid, it's been wonderful, but I've got another appointment I have to get to. I'll let you know of my final decision shortly.

Rob: Sid, that's the third backer this week.

Sid: I know, Rob, and I don't feel very optimistic about him either. I hate to tell you folks this when we've come so far and you're all doing so well, but if we don't get a backer soon, we'll have to cancel the show.

Rob: Isn't there anything we can do?

Sid: I'm afraid not, Rob. Without money, *Poe: The Musical* just can't go on. Listen, don't you folks worry about it. It's my problem to find the money, and we will find it. Why don't you all go home early. You've done enough work for tonight. *(To Rona)* I've got some more backers auditions to set up, honey, so why don't you go on home. I'll be there as soon as I can.

Rona: Love you, Music Man.

Sid: *(leaving)* Right back at ya, Poe Girl.

Rona: *(sings)*
> Poor Sid.
> Poor Sid.
> I wish there was something
> I could do.
> But who am I kid-
> -ding?
> There's only one thing
> That I could do…
>
> Think, Rona!
> Think, Rona!
> If only I hadn't
> Spent my life
> Sleeping to the top…
>
> Poor Sid.
> Poor Sid.
> Of course, I could—
> But I couldn't—
> Should I?
> I shouldn't.
> Could I?

I could…
If I did, it would help Sid…
But should I?
It's the only help I can offer…
Is it the only help I can offer?
It's the only help I can offer.
Could I?…
I could.
Should I?…
Will I?…

(Blackout.)

Music Under Scene Change.

At Rise: *(Lights come up on the hotel bar. At the piano, the PIANIST is playing Robert Schumann's* Traumerei. *SID is having an interview with MOSNI NIAC.)*

Mosni: So Sid Lexic, the eternal bachelor, is getting hitched to Rona Exic after only a month? What spurned the sudden change in attitude?

Sid: Well, to paraphrase one of my fellow musical theater song-writers, none of us can help where—or when—we may fall in love.

Mosni: Very true. So, when's the wedding planned for?

Sid: Well, Rona and I were talking about it and we both thought it would be nice to have it on the opening night of *Poe: The Musical,* after the show.

Mosni: And when will that much-anticipated date be?

Sid: Well, at the moment there is no official date set, as we currently have no backers. But assuming everything goes to schedule, we should be opening within—

(RONA bursts into the lounge overjoyed and interrupts the interview.)

Rona: I'm sorry to interrupt, darling, but I've got great news that just couldn't wait.

Sid: Well, what is it, Rona?

Rona: Well, I was…talking with Sab Tard and I convinced him to back *Poe*! He's going to give us a full backing!

Sid: *(jumping up and kissing RONA)* Rona, that's amazing! Quick, pull up a chair and I'll order a round of drinks for the three of us to celebrate.

Mosni: Well, actually, I have an appointment to make. But congratulations to you two on all accounts. I really couldn't be happier for you. I'm sure you'll be very happy together.

Sid: Well, I'm sorry you have to go, but I understand.

Mosni: Thank you. Call Bonnie and set up an appointment for an interview sometime before opening night.

Sid: The usual drill.

Mosni: Good-bye, and congratulations. *(She exits.)*

Sid: *(to BARTENDER)* Bartender! Two martinis, please! *(to RONA)* Rona, this is the best news I've heard all week! How on earth did you change Sab's mind?

Rona: *(uncomfortably)* Oh, does it really matter? All that matters is that we got the backing.

Sid: Oh, come now. Don't be modest. The man was thoroughly against backing the show, and now he's giving us a full backing. I'd love to know your secret.

Rona: Really, it's nothing important.

Sid: Come on, just tell me what you said.

Rona: Well, it doesn't have to do so much with what I said…

Sid: *(confused)* What?

Rona: Oh…you promise not to get mad?

Sid: Why would I get mad?

Rona: Well…I kind of…slept with him. *(SID turns pale with shock. By this point, the PIANIST has finished playing* Traumerei, *taken a short break, and is now playing Beethoven's* Sonata Pathetique: First Movement.*)* I'm sorry, Sid. It was the only thing I could think of to help the show. I just wanted to help and the only way I've ever known to get what I want from a man is to sleep with him.

Sid: *(in pain)* How could you?

Rona: I just did what I thought was—

Sid: *(quietly)* Out.

Rona: I didn't want to hurt you, really. I just wanted to hel—

Sid: *(yelling)* Out! Out of this lounge! Out of my life! Just get out!

Rona: *(placing her engagement ring on the table)* I am so sorry. *(Crying, she leaves the bar.)*

Bartender: *(offering the drinks to SID)* Do you still want the drinks?

(SID hurls the drinks across the room.)

Bartender: *(leaving)* They're on the house.

(SID snaps his fingers and all action in the lounge freezes except for him.)

Sid: *(sings)*
>How could she?
>How could she?
>She wouldn't!
>She did.
>She couldn't!
>She did.
>I trusted my soul in her hands.
>I thought we had found each other.
>I was a fool to think she'd understand.
>For Rona there will always be another

Man to conquer.
I had let down my barrier.
I should have known we'd end up
Like this.

Love, for me, is dead.
I was a fool when I said
"I'm in love."
At last, I finally see
Alone is the way for me.
Never again will I say
I don't want to be alone.
I would rather be alone.

(Suddenly the action unfreezes and the COMPANY enters, marching around SID as he crumples to the floor.)

Company: *(sings)*
    In all the land of Broadway
    There's one director who stands
          out among the rest
    Although we wouldn't go as far
          as to say he's the best.
    All his shows seem to say
    "Hey, look at me!
    I'm the strangest writer/director on
          Broadway today!"
    Hey, Sid Lexic,
    Yes, Sid Lexic,
    Hey, Sid Lexic,

(SID storms off stage)

Rob: Buddah, you can be a pain in the butt.

Company: *(jazz hands!)*
      Yeah!

End of Act I.

Act II

At Rise: *(It is the dress rehearsal for "Poe: The Musical." Full costumes, lighting, orchestra, etc. ROB, as usual, is sitting at a C. desk writing.)*

Chorus: *(sings)*

Hear the tolling of the bells—
Iron bells!

What a world of solemn thought their melody
compels!
In the silence of the night,
How we shiver with affright
At the melancholy menace of their tone!
For every sound that floats
From the rust within their throats
Is a groan.
And the people—ah, the people—
They that dwell up in the steeple,
All alone,
And who tolling, tolling, tolling,
In that muffled monotone,
Feel a glory in so rolling
On the human heart a stone—
They are neither man nor woman—
They are neither brute nor human—
They are Ghouls:
And their king it is who tolls;
And he rolls, rolls, rolls,
Rolls
A paean from the bells!
And his merry bosom swells
With the paean of the bells!
And he dances and he yells;
Keeping time, time, time,

In a sort of Runic Rhyme,
To the paean of the bells—
                    Of the bells:
Keeping time, time, time,
In a sort of Runic Rhyme,
To the throbbing of the bells—
Of the bells, bells, bells—
To the sobbing of the bells;
Keeping time, time, time,
As he knells, knells, knells,
In a happy Runic rhyme,
To the rolling of the bells—
                    Of the bells, bells, bells—
                    To the tolling of the bells,
Of the bells, bells, bells, bells—
                    Bells, bells, bells—
To the moaning and the
                    groaning of the bells.

(SAB walks on stage clapping. SID—back to his old, foul-tempered self—stalks up after him.)

Sab: Wonderful! Spectacularly splendid! Rona, honey, you were ravishing as always. Sid, I believe we have a hit! Do we have a hit? I believe we have a hit here. We're going to knock their hats off tomorrow night.

Sid: *(stuffily)* Sure. Yeah. Whatever. Listen up, I have some notes for you all. Rob, could you *please* try to make it look like you're actually writing. I, personally, am having a very hard time believing that you're Edgar Allan Poe.

Rob: I—

Sid: *(lashing out)* I don't want excuses, I want results. Help me help me[*]! Come on, people, work with me here! And chorus, do you think, for once, that you could hit the right notes for me? It's not that hard. You just need to—

Sab: *(interrupting)* Sid, may I have a word with you for a moment?

Sid: *(after a long, awkward pause)* Of course, Sab. *(to CAST)* This will be just a moment. *(to SAB as they walk down-stage)* Make this quick.

Sab: Do you think you could lighten up on them a bit, they're doing a good job.

Sid: Forgive me for striving for perfection, Sab.

Sab: All I'm saying is that I don't think it would hurt to offer them some encouragement, now and then.

Sid: *(breaking out)* For God's sake, will you stop interfering with my life and let me work the way *I* work!

(There is an awkward silence, as the CAST stares at them dumbfounded.)

Sab: *(tensely)* I will pretend that you didn't say that, Sid, seeing as it is obviously nothing more than pre-opening night jitters. *(to CAST)* You've all done a spectacular job, really. You can all go home and we'll see you here tomorrow at call time. Good job everyone.

---

[*] As in Act I, a play on "Help me help you."

(to RONA, as he exits U.L.) Meet you outside in ten, hon?

Rona: *(as she exits U.R.)* Sure thing, Sab.

(SID storms off U.L. The CAST lingers around on stage. Everyone is upset about SID and RONA'S breakup, with the exception of ROB who won the bet on how long it would take for SID and RONA to break up.)

Woman 1: *(music under)* Can you believe this?

Woman 2: *(music under)* Rona never should have broken up with him.

Woman 1: When they were together Sid was almost— but not entirely—completely unlike Sid.

Rob: *(scribbling on a notepad)* I don't know what you're all so upset about. By the way, seeing as I won the Sid and Rona break-up bet, I believe you all owe me some money.

Woman 1: *(sings)*
    The woman's nuts…

Woman 2: *(sings)*
    The bitch is crackers…

Ensemble: *(sings)*
    She's got some guts
    To screw us all over like that.

Rob: *(collecting his bet money)* I got no complaints!

Ensemble:
>   What was she thinking?
>   She had a good thing going
>   With Sid.
>   Sure, he can be a bit…

Solo 1: Eccentric…

Solo 2: Eclectic…

Solo 3: A dick…

Solo 4: A prick…

Solo 5: An emotional brick…

Ensemble:
>   But when he was with her
>   He was really nice to us.

Rob: *(checking his records)* Hey Caz, you still owe me five bucks!

Ensemble:
>   Hey Rona, please us!
>   Won't you help us help us?
>   Jesus!
>   Come on, Rona, help us help us!
>   Help us help us!
>   God, Rona
>   What were you thinking?

Rob: *(counting up his money)* Three hundred bucks!

(The CAST exits, fed-up. RONA creeps on stage, she has obviously heard everything they said about her.)

Rona: *(sings)*
>Most my life I've lived this way
>From day to boring day.
>Always singing the same old song…
>Have I had it all wrong?
>
>I was certain that I was right,
>But as I lay awake at night,
>I wonder if I was wrong.
>Have I been off all along?
>
>It's too late for me and Sid,
>I can't undo what I did.
>But I can start again.
>I will find my heart again.
>
>It's not too late to start anew,
>I can make a new life!
>The horizon is shining blue,
>I know I'll get through life!
>
>I'll start again, I'll love my man
>With all my heart and soul!
>I've found my song,
>At last I have a goal!
>I've really had it all wrong.

(SID enters from U.L. When he sees RONA, he turns around and starts to leave.)

Rona: Sid, wait! We need to talk.

Sid: There's nothing to talk about.

Rona: Yes, there is. We can't just go on pretending that nothing happened. Look, I'm sorry I hurt you, but—

Sid: You have no idea what you did to me. I trusted you—I *loved* you, Rona. Do you have any idea how hard it was for me to admit that to myself, let alone you? Every person I have ever trusted—every person I have ever loved, has betrayed—has hurt me in some way. Do you have any idea how hard it was for me to put all that behind me and try to move on? The only thing I've ever been is alone. I left that to be with you and you sent me back there. You can't just ask me to forget that. I'll see you at call tomorrow night.

Rona: *(as SID leaves)* You're not alone.

(Blackout.)
Music Under Scene Change.

At Rise: *(SID enters his apartment and collapses onto the couch. He checks his answering machine. The apartment is staged entirely in stage L. For now, stage R. is completely dark.)*

Sid's Mother: *(on answering machine)* Sid, this is your mother. I hear you've got another one of those shows opening tomorrow. When are you going to move on and do something useful with your life? Do you really expect to spend your life throwing out one useless musical after another? Anyway, I have to go to AA. Call me.

Sid: *(reflecting)* She never understood. My father did. After he died, mother turned to alcohol to escape from his pain. I turned to the piano to escape from her.

(Lights come up on stage R. A TEENAGE SID is diligently practicing Beethoven's Moonlight Sonata *on the piano. SID'S mother, obviously drunk, yells from off-stage.)*

Sid's Mother: Sid! Cut out that racket!

(TEENAGE SID, pretending not to hear her, ignores her and only plays louder and more passionately. SHE stumbles in and tries to get him to stop playing, but he continues to ignore her.)

Sid's Mother: I said, cut out that racket! Sid, for the last time cut out that God-damn racket!

(To get his attention, she slams the lid of the piano down on his hand, as he screams in pain, the scene fades out.)

Sid: A teacher at school noticed my broken hand, and reported that she suspected child abuse. We went to court. My mother was found incompetent to take care of me. I was placed into the care of my uncle, Eddie. Eddie provided me with a roof, spending money, and food, but not much more. His carefree bachelor lifestyle meant that I was expected to stay out of the way whenever he had a girlfriend over, which was often enough. Just about the only activity Eddie and I shared together was going to Broadway matinees. When I was eighteen, I moved out on my own, Eddie continued to help support me until I was able to support myself. I haven't spoken to my mother in over ten years...

(Blackout.)

During Scene Change:
(The QUARTET enters the spotlight.)

Quartet: *(sings)*
> It's opening night of Sid's new show,
> A musical dedication to Edgar Poe.
> Soon it might tour to your neighborhood.
> Who knows? Maybe this one will be good.

Terence: *(sings)*
> The man can't stop!
> The man can't stop!
> When will he learn
> His shows all flop?
> It makes my stomach churn,
> And makes my head burn.

Barry: *(sings)*
> The only way Sid
> Could have cast this show worse
> Would be with a cast of ducks!
> The show hasn't opened and I know it sucks!
> I wouldn't waste your bucks
> On this show that's definitely cursed.

Sophie: *(sings)*
> Like, oh my God!
> Like, oh my God!
> It's like opening night
> Of Sid's new show!

I'm like so excit-
-ed I don't know,
Like, what to do!
Maybe I should call my friends
And talk about it all night long!

Alison: *(sings)*
The question I have about *Poe: The Musical*
Is whether it's just another *Seussical*.
On occasion, Sid provides food for thought,
But I wonder if Sid should not
Have taken this up.

Quartet:
It's opening night of Sid's new show,
The cast is rearin' and ready to go!
Whether it should go on or not,
Who knows? Maybe this one will be good.

Terenc:
The man can't stop!
The man can't stop!
When will he learn
His shows all flop?
It makes my stomach churn,
And makes my head burn.

Barry: *(simultaneously w/ above)*
The only way Sid
Could have cast this show worse
Would be with a cast of ducks!
The show hasn't opened and I know it sucks!
I wouldn't waste your bucks
On this show that's definitely cursed.

Sophie: *(simultaneously w/ above)*
> Like, oh my God!
> Like, oh my God!
> It's like opening night
> Of Sid's new show!
> I'm like so excit-
> -ed I don't know,
> Like, what to do!
> Maybe I should call my friends
> And talk about it all night long!

Alison: *(simultaneously w/ above)*
> The question I have about *Poe: The Musical*
> Is whether it's just another *Seussical,*
> On occasion, Sid provides food for thought
> But I wonder if Sid should not
> Have taken this up.

Quartet:
> Maybe this one will be good!

(Blackout.)

At Rise: *(Lights come up on the opening night performance of* Poe: The Musical. *The CHORUS enters to sing the opening number,* Mister E.A. Poe. *THREE WOMEN, POE'S mistresses, stay separated from the rest of the CAST, defending POE from the CAST'S opinions of him.)*

Cast: *(sings)*
> Hey, do ya' know
> Mister E.A. Poe?

Woman 1: *(sings)*
> He's really sweet!

Woman 2: *(sings)*
> He rubs my feet!

Woman 3: *(sings)*
> I spent a night on his love seat!

Cast: When the air begins to reek
> And the walls begin to creek,
> You know that "Edgar the Freak"…

Woman 1:
> Don't call my Edgar a freak!

Cast: …Must be around!

> When you're deep in the ground you
> Find maggots around you.
> When your heart starts to pound, you
> Know Edgar has found you!

> Hey do ya' know
> Mister E.A. Poe?

Woman 1:
> He's such a dear!

Woman 2:
> He kisses my ear!

Woman 3: *(holding up a mirror)*
> He bought me a mir-
> -ror!

Cast: When the birds all stop to chirp,
And your heart pounds full of fear,
You know that "Edgar the Twerp"…

Woman 2:
Don't call him a twerp!

Cast: …Must be near!

There is no place you
Can go to hide you.
I'd be scared to face you
'Cause he's deep inside you!

Hey, do ya' know
Mister E.A. Poe?

Woman 1:
He's so cute!

Woman 2:
He's a hoot!

Woman 3:
He looks real cute in a diving suit!

Edgar knows no fear!
Edgar knows no pain!
There is no hope,
Not one ounce!
If you can't cope,
Edgar will pounce!

(A very abstract choreography sequence: mist, flashing lights, actors moving threateningly in and out of the light, etc. Throughout, the COMPANY chants "Edgar Poe" variously. At the end of the sequence, ROB appears as POE in a brilliant flash of laser lights and strobes.)

Rob: *(recites, music under)*
From childhood's hour I have not been
As others were—I have not seen
As others saw—I could not bring
My passions from a common spring.
From the same source I have not taken
My sorrow; I could not awaken
My heart to joy at the same tone;
And all I lov'd, *I* lov'd alone.
Then—in my childhood—in the dawn
Of a most stormy life—was drawn
From ev'ry depth of good and ill
The mystery which binds me still:
From the torrent or the fountain,
From the red cliff of the mountain,
From the sun that 'round me roll'd
In its autumn tint of gold—
From the lightning in the sky
As it pass'd me flying by—
From the thunder and the storm,
And the cloud that took the form
(When the rest of Heaven was blue)
Of a demon in my view.

(beat)

Rob: But all that depressing stuff aside, what would life be without women? Oh, Lenny!

(RONA parades on stage as LENORE. The THREE MISTRESSES follow her around. She and the GIRLS affectionately pet ROB as he sings.)

Rob: *(sings, doo-whop style)*   Rona & Girls:
    I gotta have girls!   Girls, girls!
    With their pretty curls!   Curly curls!
    And eyes like pearls!   Worldly pearls!
    What would life be like   Oh, please tell us!
    Without pretty girls!   No pretty girls!
    I could live without Klondike
    Bars.   Or even Milky
              Ways!

    But take out of my days   He's in quite a
              daze!
    The pretty faces in the bars   Milky Way bars!
    And life just wouldn't be worthwhile.

(The mist and dark lights return as the CAST moves back into its threatening postures.)

Cast: *(sings)*
    Hey, do ya' know
    Mister E.A. Poe?

Woman 1:
    He really cares!

Woman 2:
    He never swears!

Woman 3:
    He loves to eat pears!

Company:
>So if you care,
>You will not dare
>To mess with this Joe Shmoe.
>Please beware

Woman 3:
>Of Mister E.A. Poe!
>>*(Blackout.)*

During Scene Change:
(The QUARTET enters a spotlight and reads the reviews from their respective newspapers.)

Sophie: *(sings)*
>Sid's Lexic's new musical—

Alison: *(sings)*
>*Poe:—*

Terrence: *(sings)*
>*—The Musical—*

Barry: *(sings)*
>—stinks.

Terence:
>—made Sondheim cringe.

Alison:
>—is a sacrilege against poetry.

Sophie:
>—is super!

Alison:

    Sid never ceases to appall my sense of taste.

Barry: I preferred *I Need a Trash Can*.

Terence:

    I think Lexic should not have toned it back.

Sophie:

    Eminem says it's the best—and second
        musical he's ever seen!

Barry: Sid could have had more success if he had
        written *Bin Laden: The Musical*.

Alison:

    Sid should have never returned to minimalism.

Terence:

    It's just not something Lloyd Webber would
        write.

Sophie:

    Mister Em says he's writing a show that's based
        on the works of Shel Silversteen!

Alison:

    It was a rather unpleasant evening.

Terence:

    Completely miserable.

Barry: Unbearable.

All Four:
> I've never seen anything so…

Alison, Terence, Barry: Sophie:
> …Terrible.   …Super!

At Rise: *(The QUARTET exits as the lights come up on SID'S apartment, which, as earlier, is moved entirely into stage L. for the following scene. For now, stage R. is completely dark. As the lights come up, SID is sitting, crushed, on the couch reading the reviews of* Poe.*)*

Sid: *(sings, crushed)*
> Look at these reviews.
> Look at these reviews.
> It's the same old news.
> Can I keep on going,
> Resisting their critique?
> They won't stop snowing,
> And it's making me so weak.

(Crushed, SID checks his answering machine.)

Message #1: Hey Sid, it's Barry again. Look, you might not want to read the reviews. Just thought I'd give you a heads up. Later.

Message #2 (Mosni): Hey Sid, it's Mosni. I am so sorry. They really are being too harsh on you. Don't let their crap get to you, 'kay? Just keep doing what you do. There are people out there who are touched by your music. Don't let them down. Call me.

Message #3 (Odep Philé): Sid baby, bubby, dude! You can call me Odep Philé from DI Software, Inc. Just got back from seeing your musical. Splendid! Absolutely spectacular! I was blown away! Well, not really. Actually, *Poe* is the most God-awful piece of crap ever written for the stage—but it would make great video game music. Seriously dude, call me. I think we can make something special here. Something monumentally special. Or at least make a lot of money. Either way we come out pretty well, huh kid? Call me at 955-555-6161. Later bubby!

(SID stops the message, turns on the music box, crosses to the bar and pours himself a drink. He collapses on the couch. The phone rings and he lets the answering machine get it.)

Rona's Voice: Sid, I just called to tell you I've broken up with Sab. I don't expect you to forgive me and forget everything that happened. I know you could never do that. I just hope that you don't give up on love just because of what I did to you. I know you think that there's only one song for each of us to sing, but it's not true. You have so much to give. Don't let my stupidity ruin your life. *(beat)* Goodbye.

(The music box has stopped playing. SID begins reflecting, thinking aloud to himself.)

Sid: *(music under)* Where did I go wrong? At what point in my life did I get so off track?

(Lights come up on stage R. A YOUNG GIRL finishes playing Fur Elise. *She stands and bows for an imaginary audience. The PIANO TEACHER steps forward, patting the YOUNG GIRL on the back.)*

Piano Teacher: Good job, Janie. Well, our next performer will be Sid Lexic. Sid, will you tell us all what you will be performing.

(A YOUNG SID steps up and nervously faces the "audience.")

Young Sid: My name is Sid Lexic and I will be performing *Soul and Heart*.
>*(sings, while playing, to the horror of*
> *his piano teacher)*
>I hate this song, it's so annoying.
>I hate this song, it keeps on going
>Through my head and that is why
>I hate this song. Bad words and curses
>It's way too long. There's two more verses.
>It just keeps going on and on and on and on and
>   on and
>On and on and on and on and on and on.
>
>On and on and on and on and on and on.
>
>I hate this song. I'm not afraid to say it
>I hate this song!
>*(indicating PIANO TEACHER)*
>*She* made me play it!
>
>It is so annoying
>And it makes me feel like screaming
>I hate this song!
>So do all my friends!
>Ev'rybody sing along!
>It never ends!
>It just keeps on going
>On and on and on and on and on and

On and on and on and on and
On and on and on and
On and on and on and
On and on and on and
On and on and on and on.
I hate this song!

(Lights dim on stage R. and focus turns back on SID.)

Sid: *(reminiscing)* I hated playing the piano.

(The PIANO TEACHER steps into a spotlight.)

Piano Teacher: Sid Lexic, you'll never amount to anything if you don't practice.

(SID snaps his fingers and she disappears.)

Sid: She didn't understand. I didn't want to become a musician. I didn't want to have anything to do with music. Until my father died...

Sid's Mother: *(voice-over)* Sid! Cut out that racket!

(The following scene is pantomimed in part by the TEENAGE SID at stage R.)

Sid: My injured hand left me unable to play the piano, but I found that I could write songs by plunking out a melody with my good hand and transcribing it to note paper. As my talent developed, I began writing stage musicals in the style of the special effects extravaganzas my uncle took me to see. My first shows were produced in some community play festivals. A producer saw my work and saw possible talent,

69

agreeing to produce one of my shows on Broadway. That was when *she* came into the picture. *(GODI ESS, SID's first girlfriend, appears in the pantomime scene and lures TEENAGE SID away from the piano. They waltz slowly as SID continues to narrate.)* Godi Ess was a dream come true. The first good thing to come into my life in years. She dumped me in less than a month. *(GODI shoves a startled TEENAGE SID back to the piano and walks off with another, more studly man that has entered the scene. TEENAGE SID returns to his work at the piano.)* I was young, I was fragile. Everyone I had ever loved or trusted had betrayed me. I didn't want to be hurt anymore.

(One by one, each of SID'S critics from the past and present emerge from the darkness, taunting him with their various criticisms of his life and work. The music gradually grows more chaotic, until it bursts on the verge of insanity—as SID himself bursts on the verge of insanity.)

Piano Teacher: You'll never amount to anything if you don't practice. *(cont. ad-lib)*

Sid's Mother: Sid! Cut out that racket! *(cont. ad-lib)*

Godi: Sid, I'm leaving you for Ton Alent. *(cont. ad-lib)*

Quartet: Sid's new musical, *I Need a Trash Can* stinks!

All Critics: *(chanting)*
        Hey Sid Lexic, you're so great!
        Yes, Sid Lexic, you're so great!
        Hey, Sid Lexic, you're our guy!
        Yes, Sid Lexic, you're our guy!

But Sid Lexic, you can be a pain in the—

Sid: *(breaking down, he lashes out)* Out!!!

(The CRITICS disappear into the darkness.)

(Blackout.)
Music Under Scene Change.

At Rise: *(A month has passed. SID is having an interview with MOSNI at their usual bar. The PIANIST is playing Robert Schumann's* Traumerei.*)*

Mosni: *(music under)* So, tell me what's new in the world of Sid Lexic.

Sid: Well, I've decided to establish my own non-profit theater company, La Cucaracha Theater Company.

Mosni: You named your company after a cockroach?

Sid: Well, yes. I've always believed that the best intention is the one to confuse.

Mosni: Very interesting outlook. And where will this company be based?

Sid: My uncle Eddie owns some land in a small town called Absidy, which he has agreed to lease to me. There will be two auditoriums and several recital/lecture halls. Over the summer we'll hold theater and acting workshops for the community. Our emphasis will be on producing abstract musical theater shows and providing a venue for young musical theater composers

71

to have their works produced. My cousin lives there with his wife – she's a model.

Mosni: Well, it looks like you're doing well for yourself.

Sid: Well yes, Mosni, I guess you could say that. I realized that I need to keep more of an open mind for life. I always thought Broadway was the only place I could belong in the musical theater world, but it was just the opposite. Broadway is the place I don't belong. I finally realized that there's more than one song that you can sing.

Mosni: Well I guess the future is looking bright for you, isn't it?

Sid: Yes, Mosni, it is.

(beat)

Mosni: *(rising)* Well, I guess that's a wrap for now. Be sure to keep in touch, Sid, wherever life leads you.

Sid: *(quickly)* Uh, Mosni...would you care to have dinner with me? Unless, of course, you have a prior commitment.

Mosni: Sid Lexic, I would be honored.

(He rises and they leave together.)

Finis.

About the Composer/Composer
Leinad Ekim

Leinad Ekim was born and raised on a South Carolina chicken farm by Liam and Nelly Ekim. Growing up on a chicken farm was a major influence on his life. Up to the day of his death, he still to felt sick whenever he saw someone eating Chicken McNuggets.

Although he was not brought up religiously, as a teenager he worked in a nearby church as a night janitor. To kill time during those late night shifts, he taught himself to play the church's pipe organ. The neighbors of the church weren't too happy about this young man's midnight explorations into the world of cacophony, and he was quickly relieved of his duties.

Upon his removal from the House of God, he begged his parents to buy him a pipe organ so that he could continue his cacophonic studies. Unfortunately, the chicken raising business didn't bring in quite enough money to buy a pipe organ. Plus, there wasn't much room for a pipe organ in their small farm and his parents had read that organ music makes chickens sterile. So he had to settle for a small electronic keyboard. In the end, this worked out better for everyone because Leinad could practice his cacophony without disturbing the chickens'—or his parents'—breeding rituals.

At the age of 17, his curious mind wondered what it would be like to run away from home. After discussing his inspiration with his puzzled parents, he upped and left for Boston Massachusetts, promising his parents to send them a post card. Upon Leinad's departure, Liam Ekim turned to his wife and said, "Well Nelly, at least we know for certain that the boy's cracked in the head. We should have known better when we named him."

Although his parents had no way of knowing it at the time, the real reason Leinad was leaving was not a thirst for knowledge. Leinad was becoming very sick. In Boston he saw several doctors and none of them knew what was wrong with him. Eventually, it was decided that Leinad had contracted a genetic disorder so rare that he was the first person ever to get it. Essentially, Leinad had become allergic to physical human contact.

The only human contact Leinad could make was over the phone or through chat rooms on-line. Which is how he met and befriended Mike Daniel who, at the time, was in his senior year of high school getting ready to move to Boston to go to Berklee College of Music. Upon hearing Leinad's bizarre musical style, Mike asked Leinad if he would like to compose the music for a musical adaptation of Washington Irving's *Sleepy Hollow*. Leinad eagerly agreed and the duo began their first collaboration. "It's not an easy collaboration process," Mike was once quoted as saying. "Because of Leinad's illness, we can't meet in person, we have to send each other stuff by e-mail. To complicate things further, I was doing the orchestrations for the show since Leinad had no experience writing for the orchestra. I'd e-mail him my lyrics, he'd e-mail me back the music, I'd write out the orchestrations and e-mail them back to him for his approval. It took about a month to write one song."

After the September 11th attacks, Mike suggested to Leinad that they collaborate on a *Requiem* in honor of the victims of terrorism. Leinad eagerly agreed and they set to work, incorporating some of Mike's music from *Frankenstein* and some of Leinad's music from *Sleepy Hollow*. As with Sleepy Hollow, the entire collaboration had to take place on line. Their next collaboration was an original musical "dramedy," *Alone*. For this show, the duo agreed that it would be easiest if Mike collaborated on some of the music.

Tragically, Leinad Ekim committed suicide on the opening night of *Alone*. He ordered a pair of identical twin call girls. The extreme degree of physical contact triggered an allergic reaction and he fell into a coma, dying a few hours later. "When he started shaking and all, we just thought he was enjoying it," one of the call girls was quoted as saying. "Then he went all stiff…and not in the good way…" Before his tragic, if somewhat interesting, demise, Leinad left this last, final, message to the world:

"Cruel, tragic world, I leave you now on this, the happiest night of my life. Tonight, my music will meet the world for the first time. Tonight, I ate a gigantic pizza with extra pepperoni and stuffed crust. I also had two root beer floats. Oh yeah, and tonight I will get laid. I can honestly think of no better way to go out. I have left more than enough music on my six computers for Mike to publish over the next several years (This will be news to Mike. What can I say, I like surprises). Please do not mourn my passing any more than you would mourn my passing gas. And besides, maybe I'll get a Pulitzer Prize now. After all, it worked for Johnathan Larson. Foibly yours, Leinad Ekim"

Leinad's biography is longer than Mike's because his life-story was more interesting.

About the Composer/Lyricist
Mike Daniel

Mike Daniel was born and raised in Kailua-Kona, Hawaii. He received his B.M. (Bachelor of Music, you dirty-minded filth) in Film Scoring from Berklee College of Music in Boston, Massachusetts and his Masters in Film Music Composition from the North Carolina School of the Arts.

He is the composer/librettist of the musicals *Frankenstein* and *The Show Must Go On*. *Sleepy Hollow* was his first collaboration as librettist with composer Leinad Ekim. Together, they have also written a *Requiem* in honor of the victims of terrorism and an original musical "dramedy," *Alone*. Mike wishes Leinad had discussed the details of his six computers that Mike is now in charge of before choosing the path of climactic death.

Mike's biography is shorter than Leinad's because Mike doesn't enjoy talking about himself as much.

Note From the Composer/Lyricist

I am speaking for myself when I say that *Alone* is in no way, shape, or form, autobiographical. It goes without saying that *Alone* isn't biographical for Leinad, due to his disease. (Those of you who aren't aware of Leinad's disease, are obviously not the type of people who read the author biographies. Otherwise, you would know every single uncomfortable detail about Leinad's disease as well as other aspects of his life that most of us don't really want to know. Of course, those of you who aren't the type of people to read the author biographies, most likely aren't the type of people to read the author notes, so what am I talking to *you* for? Those of you who are the type to read the author biographies and just haven't gotten around to it yet, I would strongly suggest that you read Leinad's before continuing. Otherwise it is highly possible that I might confuse you. And I most certainly wouldn't want that to happen…neppah ot taht tnaw *dluow* ylniatrec tsom I.)

Naturally, there are certain aspects of our respective attitudes and outlooks on life which have creeped into Sid's character. However, on the whole Sid is an entirely fictitious character. My parents were not abusive alcoholics, I had very pleasant piano teachers when I was growing up (although I *did* hate practicing…), and—at the time of this writing—I have never been adopted by a rich uncle. Leinad's parents were very loving chicken farmers, he is a self-taught musician (don't you *hate* those guys?) so he never took music lessons, and although he does have a rich uncle, they're only related through an incestuous marriage, so it doesn't really count.

With that out of the way, I'd like to discuss some feedback I've received regarding one of the songs from this show. A lot of people come have come up to me while I'm jogging through the park and told me that Rona's first song in the show, *British Desserts*, is a dirty song. I am, quite honestly, puzzled by this reaction. *British Desserts* is just a perfectly innocent song about a young woman who loves an unfortunately named dessert called the "Spotted Dick" (This is a real dessert served in England. Don't believe me? Check it out on the web.) I personally don't think it's fair of people to blame me for the fact that they have sick minds. I will, however, take full responsibility for the amount of B.S. in this paragraph.

I have one thing to say regarding the ending. It is intentionally vague. Leinad and I considered ending it with a big happy musical number between Mosni and Sid, but decided that was not what we were going for. *Alone* is not a traditional musical comedy, it is a musical dramedy—a dramatic musical with some comedic moments along the way. The moment at the end is not about Sid and Mosni finally getting together after all this time, the moment at the end is about Sid opening up to new experiences. The point here is that life is not a musical, the play isn't over when the audience goes home—whether Sid and Mosni live happily ever after in a castle on a cloud is irrelevant and should be decided by each individual person.

Mike Daniel
Boston, Massachusetts
12/19/02

www.ingramcontent.com/pod-product-compliance
Lightning Source LLC
Chambersburg PA
CBHW020514030426
42337CB00011B/377